JESUS ON TRIAL

JESUS ON TRIAL

James Montgomery Boice

Philip Graham Ryken

CROSSWAY BOOKS

A DIVISION OF
GOOD NEWS PUBLISHERS
WHEATON, ILLINOIS

Jesus on Trial

Copyright © 2002 by Linda McNamara Boice and Philip Graham Ryken

Published by Crossway Books

    a division of Good News Publishers

    1300 Crescent Street

    Wheaton, Illinois 60187

Cover design: Cindy Kiple

First printing 2002

Printed in the United States of America

Library of Congress Cataloging-in-Publication Data

Boice, James Montgomery, 1938–2000

  Jesus on trial / James Montgomery Boice, Philip Graham Ryken ; with a foreword by David A. Skeel, Jr.

    p.   cm.

  Includes bibliographical references and index.

  ISBN 1-58134-401-5 (alk. paper)

  1. Jesus Christ—Trial. I. Ryken, Philip Graham, 1966– II. Title.

BT440 .B64   2002

232.96'2—dc21   2001008181

                                        CIP

15	14	13	12	11	10	09	08	07	06	05	04	03	02
15	14	13	12	11	10	9	8	7	6	5	4	3	2	1

TRIAL

A judicial examination and determination, in accordance with the law of the land, of a case, either civil or criminal, of the issues between the parties, whether of law or fact, before a court that has proper jurisdiction.

Black's Law Dictionary

APR 2002

CONTENTS

FOREWORD

Trials can be riveting, as writers and movie makers have always known. For example, the novels of Charles Dickens give us a vivid picture of the legal system in Victorian England. In our own era, we have movies with titles like *Witness* and *The Verdict*. Nearly all of us have seen movies about trials, read a novel by John Grisham or Scott Turow, or watched one of the many television series depicting lawyers and trials.

It is not hard to understand why we find trials so fascinating. Trials are full of suspense and drama. The police must locate and arrest the suspect before he can be brought to trial. The prosecutor must assemble witnesses and evidence, and at the trial he must match wits with the defendant's attorney as both attorneys try to persuade a jury of ordinary citizens that the defendant is guilty or innocent.

The crucifixion of Jesus Christ followed a trial that was more sensational than even the most spellbinding legal dramas of our time. This kind of event today would be front-page news from start to finish. People all over the world would talk about the witnesses, the evidence, and the defendant's strangely calm demeanor in the face of incredible charges.

As spectacular and important as it was, and although we are familiar with Jesus' arrest and crucifixion, many of us know little or nothing about his trial. Why is this? I suspect the main reason is that we tend to think that the trial was simply a sham from start to finish. We assume that Christ's enemies could have executed him for any or no reason, and thus that the trial did not serve any real purpose.

In reality, this was not the case at all. The religious leaders who arrested Jesus could not execute him themselves. Only Rome could do this. This is why Jesus' trial actually involved two trials, a trial under Jewish law followed by a Roman trial before Pontius Pilate. The religious leaders needed to follow their own proper legal procedures, and Pilate too showed a surprising concern for the requirements of Roman law.

This book is one of the few I know that focuses on the astonishing events of Jesus' trial. As you will quickly realize, the book is clearly and beautifully written. Although Drs. Boice and Ryken are both well known as theologians, each has the gift of simple, elegant expression.

The authors give careful attention to each stage of the trial, from Jesus' arrest to his execution a few hours later. Throughout the book, they provide crucial details about the requirements of ancient Jewish and Roman law. We learn, for instance, why the religious leaders were so desperate to find two witnesses with the same accusation against Jesus.

Boice and Ryken also put the trial into a contemporary perspective. Their translation of ancient legal requirements into contemporary terms may, in fact, be the book's most remarkable contribution. Each chapter provides a clear current definition of the issue under consideration. And throughout the book, the authors give incisive and helpful reminders of how Jewish law and Roman law compare to our own legal system. They explain that the plot to arrest Jesus would quite literally constitute a conspiracy under current law, and that the religious and political leaders denied Jesus proper process by trying him the night of his arrest.

I am amazed by the relevance of Jesus' trial to the kinds of questions that law professors ponder each day. Our own justice system sometimes seems to focus so much on procedural issues such as what kinds of searches the police can and cannot do that we lose sight of the substance of the issues at hand. We fail to see whether we're punishing the right person or whether the crime charged is really a crime in the first place. Like Jesus' accusers, we forget to ask what justice requires. What should a just legal system look like? How might we alter the legal system to better promote justice?

The authors' vivid account also draws us into the trial itself. As you read the book, you will feel like a juror, and indeed, that is what each of us is. We each must weigh the evidence and consider whether justice was done. To grapple with these questions is to ask who Jesus Christ was, what he did, and why he died.

Serving as a juror is only the first of our roles. As Drs. Boice and Ryken point out, God could have stopped the trial at any time. Jesus himself made this clear when he chastised Peter, saying, "Do you think I cannot call on my Father, and he will at once put at my disposal more than twelve legions of angels?" (Matt. 26:53). The God who has power over all things was watching over every aspect of the arrest and trial of Jesus. This means that the very people who served as Jesus' judges and jury—the religious leaders who conspired against Jesus and the Roman governor who allowed his execution to go forward—were themselves being judged. They were defendants too.

And so are we all. As you read this book, you will learn

everything you need to know to serve as a juror in a two-thousand-year-old trial. You will understand who Jesus was, and what it meant for him to acknowledge his claim to be "Christ, the Son of the Blessed One" (Mark 14:61), the only way of salvation. You will hear the evidence and weigh the testimony. As you fulfill this solemn charge, you must never forget that there is another trial going on at the same time, a trial before the God of all eternity. In this trial, you are the defendant and not the jury.

What does the evidence say? What is the verdict?

David A. Skeel, Jr., J.D.
University of Pennsylvania Law School
October 2001

PREFACE

In 1996 the late James Montgomery Boice and I agreed to preach a series of special sermons at Tenth Presbyterian Church in Philadelphia, where we both served as ministers. On the seven Fridays before Easter we hosted lunchtime services at our Center City church. These services began and ended with beautiful music; in between, the two of us presented short messages based on the Bible. Students, workers, church members, and friends came from nearby buildings and other parts of the city to attend. The services, which we called the Friday Lunch Easter Series, culminated with Tenth's annual Good Friday service.

That first year we called our series "Famous Last Words," and focused on the seven sayings of Christ from the cross. The next year we preached on "The *Real* Last Words of Christ," what Jesus said after he was raised from the dead. This was followed by a series based on New Testament texts that explain "The Message of the Cross." Together these twenty-one sermons were published in a Crossway book entitled *The Heart of the Cross.*

Expecting our work to continue, Dr. Boice and I began another three-year cycle of messages. In 2000 we taught on seven important aspects of the trial of Jesus Christ: the diabolical *conspiracy* to kill him; his night-time *arrest* in the Garden of Gethsemane; the short *resistance* that the disciples mounted in his defense; the *witnesses* who accused him of blasphemy during his ecclesiastical trial before the Jewish Sanhedrin; the *verdict* reached in his civil trial by the Roman governor Pontius Pilate; the *sentence* of death that his enemies demanded; and his *execution* by crucifixion. (The words in italics correspond to the seven chapters of the present book.)

Sadly, as you will learn in the "Afterword," our plans to develop this legal theme still further were cut short by Dr. Boice's sudden death from cancer in June 2000. This loss brought our collaboration to an end, and for a time the project lay dormant. However, rereading the original manuscript showed that the first seven messages were complete in themselves, and thus they are presented here as a book in their own right. Dr. Boice contributed chapters 4, 6, and 7. I wrote the other chapters and edited the final manuscript.

I thank God for the extraordinary privilege of preaching

and writing with James Boice. If he were still with us today, he would join me in praising God for the many friends who have supported the Friday Lunch Easter Series. I am also grateful for those who helped complete this book: Mr. Thomas Blackburn, who tracked down the correct legal definitions; Mrs. Linda Boice, who shared my desire to see the sermons published; Dr. Stephen Master, who reviewed the book in draft form; Ms. Patricia Russell, who prepared the indexes; Professor David Skeel, who provided the proper legal perspective; and the fine staff at Crossway, who worked hard to produce it in a timely fashion.

This book is dedicated to the God who "loves justice" (Ps. 11:7), and to his Son Jesus Christ, who "in his humiliation . . . was deprived of justice" (Acts 8:33), but who was "raised to life for our justification" (Rom. 4:25).

Philip Graham Ryken
Tenth Presbyterian Church
October 2001

CONSPIRACY

A person is guilty of conspiracy with another person or persons to commit a crime if, with intent of promoting or facilitating its commission, he agrees with such other person or persons that they or one or more of them will engage in conduct which constitutes such crime.

PENNSYLVANIA CODE 18 PA.C.S.A. § 903(A)

THE CONSPIRACY

The philosopher Plato once imagined what would happen if a perfect man ever came to live on this imperfect planet. The kind of person Plato had in mind would be "a just man in his simplicity and nobleness," willing to hold on to his "course of justice unwavering to the point of death." The great philosopher could well imagine what would happen to such a man in this wicked world: "Our just man will be thrown into prison, scourged and racked, will have his eyes burnt out, and, after every kind of torment, be impaled."[1]

Without realizing it, Plato described Jesus of Nazareth, also called Christ. For Jesus was a just man, a man of noble simplicity who maintained his justice to the point of death.

And he was treated the way Plato expected. Jesus was arrested, tortured, and executed. Furthermore, Jesus was put to death in precisely the manner Plato indicated. He was impaled on a tree; or, as the custom was in those days, he was crucified.

Jesus was treated shamefully. The only perfect man who ever lived was physically abused and brutally murdered. From a legal standpoint, the whole thing was a travesty, the greatest miscarriage of justice in the history of the world. Yet, strangely, it was all done in the name of justice. Jesus was professionally arrested, formally tried, judicially condemned, and officially executed. When Jesus was put on trial, many of the proper legal procedures were followed. The question is, Where did it all go wrong? How did an innocent man end up dying like a common criminal?

IN THE PALACE OF CAIAPHAS

Before the trial of Jesus, there was a conspiracy. The whole sordid, scandalous affair began with a perverse group of men who were jealous of Jesus: "Then the chief priests and the elders of the people assembled in the palace of the high priest, whose name was Caiaphas, and they plotted to arrest Jesus in some sly way and kill him. 'But not during the Feast,' they said, 'or there may be a riot among the people'" (Matt. 26:3-5).

These conspirators were some of the most highly respected men in Jerusalem. The "chief priests" were religious leaders; probably they were the ones who "opened the meeting in prayer." In a way, they were also lawyers—experts in God's law. The "elders of the people" were the political leaders. They were members of the Sanhedrin, the ruling council of the Jewish people. Together these priests and politicians formed an unholy alliance. Their aim was not simply to discredit Jesus but to do away with him altogether.

The proper legal term for the meeting they held in the palace of Caiaphas is "conspiracy." According to the law of the Commonwealth of Pennsylvania, "A person is guilty of conspiracy with another person or persons to commit a crime if, with intent of promoting or facilitating its commission, he agrees . . . that . . . one or more of them will engage in conduct which constitutes such crime or . . . solicitation to commit such crime."[2] These men did the latter. They solicited an assassination. Their intent was to commit murder, but Jerusalem was crowded with worshipers, and Jesus was much too popular to attack in public, so they needed to be discreet.

Their opportunity to act came from the most unexpected quarter. One of Jesus' closest disciples, "one of the Twelve—the one called Judas Iscariot—went to the chief priests and asked, 'What are you willing to give me if I hand him over to you?'" (Matt. 26:14-15a). The Jewish leaders probably would have paid almost anything to get their hands on Jesus. "So they counted out for him thirty silver coins. From then on Judas watched for an opportunity to hand him over" (Matt. 26:15b-16). Thus Judas became the most infamous traitor in history, and the Son of God was sold for thirty pieces of silver.

Why did they do it? What was it about Jesus that led these men to hate him? It is not certain why Judas betrayed Jesus. He may have been disillusioned. Perhaps he was looking for a Messiah who would overthrow the Romans and bring the Jews back to political power. Or perhaps he was simply greedy. After all, Judas served as the treasurer for Jesus and his disciples. There was nothing he liked better than the sound of silver coins clinking together in his bag (John 12:5-6). Whatever the reason for his treachery, it was a total sellout.

In the case of the political leaders, it may have had something to do with Jesus' popularity. Just a few days earlier, Jesus had entered Jerusalem riding on a donkey. Tens of thousands had lined the streets, waving palm branches and welcoming him as their rightful king. The elders knew that they could never hope to compete with such a charismatic figure.

Jesus was dangerous to them because he threatened their authority.

The religious leaders hated Jesus because he had a knack for exposing their secret sins. Whenever Jesus taught about hypocrisy, which was frequently, they had the sneaking suspicion that he was talking about them, and usually they were right about this (Matt. 21:45). They also hated Jesus because he claimed to be God. Since they refused to believe that he was the divine Lord, they thought that he was a false prophet, and in those days blasphemy was punishable in Jewish law by death (see Lev. 24:13-16). They were wrong, of course. Jesus really *was* God! If they needed proof, all they needed to do was witness his miracles, but they had already concluded that he was a fraud.

WHO'S TO BLAME?

It is an irrefutable fact of history that Jesus was brought to trial by the leaders of the Jewish faith. The men who hatched the conspiracy against him were among the highest ranking officials in Israel. It is also true that they took full responsibility for their own actions. Later, when the Roman governor tried to talk them out of having Jesus crucified, they said, "Let his blood be on us and on our children!" (Matt. 27:25).

Yet it would be a mistake to blame the Jews alone for the crucifixion. Much evil has come from the idea that "the Jews killed Jesus," not least in Nazi Germany. Therefore, it is important to see how many other people were implicated in this conspiracy. An Idumean king named Herod handed Jesus over to the Romans. A Roman governor named Pontius Pilate ordered Jesus to be crucified. Roman soldiers carried out Pilate's orders, nailing Jesus to a wooden cross and hanging him up to die. The Jews brought Jesus to trial, but in the end the Gentiles killed him.

These facts are significant because they show how the whole human race was implicated in the conspiracy against God's one and only Son. The Jews could not have killed Jesus without the Gentiles, for they did not have the right under Roman law to execute capital punishment, even though their religious law could punish blasphemy with death. Nor would the Gentiles have considered killing him without the Jews, for they had no real quarrel with Jesus. From the conspiracy to the execution, the trial of Jesus depended on an unlikely coalition of Jews and Gentiles. In the words of Vinoth Ramachandra, "Jesus was condemned to death, not by the irreligious and the uncivilized, but by the highest representatives of Jewish religion and Roman law."[3]

This shows that every one of us belongs to a sinful race. Are we any better than the men who put Jesus to death? "Not at all!" the Bible says. "Jews and Gentiles alike are all under sin. As it is written:

> 'There is no one righteous, not even one;
>   there is no one who understands,
>   no one who seeks God.
> All have turned away,
>   they have together become worthless;
> There is no one who does good,
>   not even one'" (Rom. 3:9-12).

If no one is righteous (not even one!) then we too are among the accused.

One man who understood his own personal rebellion against Christ was the composer Johann Sebastian Bach. In a dramatic moment in Bach's *St. John Passion,* Jesus is struck by the servants of the high priest. This episode is recorded in the Bible: "They spit in his face and struck him with their fists. Others slapped him and said, 'Prophesy to us, Christ. Who hit you?'" (Matt. 26:67-68). At this point it would have been customary for a composer—especially a German one—to blame the whole scene on the Jews. But Bach gave a different answer. He identified himself with sinful humanity.

"Who is it that has hit you?" the choir asks. "I, I and my sins," is the response. Bach understood that, in a very real sense, it was his own sins that led Christ to suffer and to die.

The artist Stanley Spencer, who often painted biblical scenes set in his native English village, also understood this. In one painting Spencer gave a whole new perspective on the crucifixion. The cross itself is at the center of the painting, but it is viewed from behind, with the figure of Christ obscured. The viewer's attention is drawn not to Christ himself but to those who are fixing him to the cross, carrying out the messy business of crucifixion. Who are the executioners? They are ordinary people from the artist's hometown, wearing the grubby clothes and brewery caps of common laborers. The point of Spencer's painting is that Jesus was crucified by ordinary people—sinners just like us.

Since every human being is a sinner, each one of us is implicated in the conspiracy against God's Son. Are you willing to confess your own complicity? The poet Jacob Revius made his confession in the form of a sonnet entitled "He Bore Our Griefs":

> No, it was not the Jews who crucified,
> Nor who betrayed You in the judgment place,
> Nor who, Lord Jesus, spat into Your face,

Nor who with buffets struck You as You died.

No, it was not the soldiers fisted bold
Who lifted up the hammer and the nail,
Or raised the cursed cross on Calvary's hill,
Or, gambling, tossed the dice to win Your robe.

I am the one, O Lord, who brought You there,
I am the heavy cross You had to bear,
I am the rope that bound You to the tree,

The whip, the nail, the hammer, and the spear,
The blood-stained crown of thorns You had to wear:
It was my sin, alas, it was for me.[4]

THE DIVINE CONSPIRACY

The strangest thing of all is that God himself was in on the conspiracy. God not only allowed Jesus to be put on trial but also planned for him to be crucified. God knew that it was only through the atoning death of Jesus that sinners could find forgiveness and receive eternal life. Call it the "divine conspiracy"—a holy God conspiring to save guilty humanity.

When explaining the crucifixion, the first disciples made it clear that Jesus' death was part of God's plan. To the Jewish leaders who had Jesus killed, they said, "This man was handed over to you by God's set purpose and foreknowledge; and you, with the help of wicked men [in other words, the Romans], put him to death by nailing him to the cross. But God raised him from the dead. . . . God has made this Jesus, whom you crucified, both Lord and Christ" (Acts 2:23-24, 36). The followers of Christ were not afraid to blame Jews and Gentiles alike for the wrongful death of God's own Son, but they also emphasized the deeper conspiracy, that God was plotting to use their dastardly deed to accomplish his salvation.

Jesus was in on the conspiracy too. He said as much to his disciples. He said it almost casually, as if it were the most natural thing in the world: "As you know," Jesus said, "the Son of Man will be handed over to be crucified" (Matt. 26:2). This was more than a prediction; it was a prophecy. The crucifixion was part of God's plan for saving sinners, and Jesus was in on the plan. He knew that he would be "handed over"— that is to say, handed over by the Jews—"to be crucified" by the Romans. He also knew that his death would mean forgiveness and salvation for everyone who trusts in him.

Many of those who conspired against Jesus later discovered this for themselves. The moment Jesus died there was an earthquake, and the Roman soldiers who were guarding the cross said, "Surely he was the Son of God!" (Matt. 27:54). Many of the Jewish priests reached the same conclusion. Once Jesus was safely crucified, they assumed they would never have to deal with him again. But they were wrong. Three days later Jesus rose from the dead, showing his disciples that he had conquered death once and for all. The Bible says that in the months after Jesus was raised, "a large number of priests became obedient to the faith" (Acts 6:7). Remarkable! Many of the Jews who had conspired to kill Jesus, as well as the Gentiles who actually crucified him, eventually came to worship Jesus as their God and Savior.

Jesus is just full of surprises. Put him to death, and he comes back to life. Conspire against him, seeking his death, and he will conspire against you, dying for your sins and then rising again to give you eternal life. Put Jesus on trial—if you dare! Try to decide if he measures up to your standards and you will discover that all the while *he* has been investigating *you*. Perhaps even now Jesus is plotting to bring you into a whole new relationship with him. The whole thing is a conspiracy!

ARREST

To deprive a person of his liberty by legal authority. Taking, under real or assumed authority, custody of another for the purpose of holding or detaining him to answer a criminal charge or civil demand.

BLACK'S LAW DICTIONARY

THE ARREST

It all started with the conspiracy. The highest-ranking Jewish officials plotted to bring Jesus to trial. The conspiracy led to the arrest, for before Jesus could be interrogated he had to be incarcerated. So a "detachment of soldiers with its commander and the Jewish officials arrested Jesus. They bound him and brought him first to Annas, who was the father-in-law of Caiaphas, the high priest that year" (John 18:12-13).

The arrest took place in the dead of night. After sharing his Last Supper with some of his closest friends, Jesus offered a lengthy prayer for their blessing. "When he had finished praying, Jesus left with his disciples and crossed the Kidron Valley. On the other side there was an olive grove, and he and his disciples went into it" (John 18:1). There in the quiet of the garden, Jesus was betrayed by one of his closest companions, Judas Iscariot: "Now Judas, who betrayed him, knew the place, because Jesus had often met there with his disciples. So Judas came to the grove, guiding a detachment of soldiers and some officials from the chief priests and Pharisees. They were carrying torches, lanterns and weapons" (John 18:2-3). This midnight encounter between Jesus and his enemies—both Jews and Romans—helps us understand who Jesus was and what he was doing.

THE GOD-MAN

Let's start with who Jesus was. At one level, he was a man just like any other, a human being, flesh and blood. And like any other person, he had a name. When Jesus heard his enemies enter the garden, he "went out and asked them, 'Who is it you want?'" They answered that they were looking for "Jesus of Nazareth" (John 18:4-5).

That name—Jesus of Nazareth—identified Jesus with the village of his childhood. He was born in Bethlehem, the City of David (Luke 2:1-7). For a few years he lived in Egypt, where his parents went into hiding when they feared that their son's life was in danger (Matt. 2:13-15). But eventually the family returned to Israel and settled in Nazareth (Matt. 2:19-23), which became Jesus' hometown, the place where he grew from a child to a man while working with his father, Joseph the carpenter. This rather ordinary upbringing reminds us that Jesus is a man.

Jesus is also God. This is the great mystery that Christians call the doctrine of the incarnation. It means that Jesus is fully God as well as fully man. He has both a divine nature and a human nature. He is the God-man. Like many things in Christianity, this is much easier to state than it is to understand. But that is to be expected. If God is infinite, we should expect to find that there are some aspects of his being that elude our grasp. As mere mortals, how can we wrap our minds around an eternal God?

Something happened during Jesus' arrest that demonstrated his deity. When the scribes and soldiers stated whom they were looking for, the man from Nazareth said, "I am he." "When Jesus said, 'I am he,' they drew back and fell to the ground" (John 18:5-6). Obviously, the members of this unruly posse were afraid of Jesus. But why did they fall down? They were armed soldiers surrounding an unarmed man. How could mere words be powerful enough to knock them to the ground? Obviously, there must be more to this than meets the ear.

The original Greek of the New Testament helps us understand what really happened. Jesus actually said, not "I am he," but simply "I am" (*ego eimi*), quoting two little words from one of the most important episodes in the Old Testament. The words "I AM" first appear in Exodus 3, the story of Moses at the burning bush. Moses, tending his sheep near Horeb, the mountain of God, saw a strange sight: a flaming bush that was not being consumed by the fire. As he investigated, Moses encountered the holy God. When Moses asked for some identification, God simply said, "I AM WHO I AM" (Ex. 3:14). From that time forward, the mysterious name "I AM" became the special name the Jews used for the God of Israel. It is a form of the Hebrew verb "to be." It means that God has no past and no future, only an eternal present. He is who he is; he always has been who he is; and he always will be who he is.

When Jesus confronted his captors, saying, "I am," he was quoting God's words to Moses. By doing so, he claimed to be the eternal God, personally appropriating the unique divine name of the Lord God of Israel. Jesus used that special name with such authority that for a moment his enemies were driven back in terror. Perhaps they even caught a glimpse of his divine glory. In his comments on this passage, the Scottish preacher Alexander Maclaren wrote, "I am inclined to think that here . . . there was for a moment a little rending of the veil of his flesh, and an emission of some flash of the brightness that always tabernacled within him. . . . [T]he one stray beam of manifest divinity that shot through the crevice, as it were, for an instant, was enough to prostrate with a strange awe even those rude and insensitive men."[1] If Maclaren is right, it certainly would explain why Jesus' enemies fell to the ground: they had seen and heard God in his glory.

Here we encounter the paradox of the incarnation. Even at a moment of apparent weakness, when Jesus seems to be a defenseless victim at the mercy of dangerous men, he is still the God of all power and glory. Who is Jesus? The man from Nazareth is God incarnate, the great I AM, the glorious and eternal Lord.

VOLUNTARY SURRENDER

Since Jesus is both man and God, he could see it all coming. He went to meet his captors knowing full well "all that was going to happen to him" (John 18:4). He knew that he would be not only unlawfully arrested but also unfairly tried, unjustly convicted, and unmercifully crucified. All this makes it impossible not to conclude that Jesus surrendered to this arrest of his own free will. No matter how heavily armed they were, his enemies never could have apprehended him unless he allowed them to do so.

These men had tried to arrest Jesus several times before, but had failed. John mentions three such occasions in his Gospel. The first time, a group of temple guards tried to arrest Jesus because people were claiming that he was the Christ. But the guards never managed to lay a hand on him. When they returned to their leaders and were questioned as to why they had failed to bring Jesus in, they simply shrugged their shoulders and said, "No one ever spoke the way this man does" (John 7:46).

A second arrest attempt failed after Jesus explicitly claimed to be God, saying, "I tell you the truth, before Abraham was born, I am!" (John 8:58). As we have seen, saying "I am" was one way that Jesus announced his deity. Thinking this was blasphemy, the religious leaders "picked up stones to stone him, but Jesus hid himself, slipping away from the temple grounds" (John 8:59). And on a similar occasion, while Jesus was at the temple in Jerusalem claiming to be God the Son, "again they tried to seize him, but he escaped their grasp" (John 10:39).

On at least three separate occasions, then, it had proved impossible to arrest Jesus. This is one of the reasons Judas was so essential to the conspiracy. Only an informer like Judas would know when and where to catch Jesus. It may also explain why they went so heavily armed. In his famous book on the last week of Christ's life, the journalist Frank Morison points out that "in all their dealings with Jesus, these men were apprehensive of something happening that they did not care to define. They seem to have been in some doubt whether even a considerable force would be adequate to take Him, and that in the last moment He might even prove to be unarrestable."[2]

Thus Jesus' enemies faced a problem of unusual difficulty. They were trying to arrest the world's most dangerous man! The religious leaders were much too afraid of Jesus to take any chances with him. They had heard of his miraculous powers, and they knew that previous attempts to arrest him had ended in failure. Besides, they may have said, how do you incarcerate a man who claims to be God? He might be mad. He might do anything. He might even hurt us. So their only solution was to ambush him by night.

All their preparations were irrelevant, of course. If Jesus had wanted to elude their grasp once again, or even to overpower them, he could have done so in an instant. The obvious implication is that his surrender was purely voluntary. The whole thing was a divine conspiracy, remember, and Jesus was in on it. Earlier, when he had first started speaking about his sufferings and death, he had raised and responded to a rhetorical question: "Now my heart is troubled, and what shall I say? 'Father, save me from this hour'? No, it was for this very reason I came to this hour" (John 12:27). Jesus came to suffer and to die for our sins, and the first step was to surrender to his arrest.

SAFE IN CHRIST

Ordinarily, when a man is about to be arrested, his first thought is for his own safety. But Jesus' primary concern was for the safety of his friends. After his enemies had picked themselves up off the ground,

> Again he asked them, "Who is it you want?"
> And they said, "Jesus of Nazareth."
> "I told you that I am he," Jesus answered. "If you are looking for me, then let these men go." This happened so that the words he had spoken would be fulfilled: "I have not lost one of those you gave me" (John 18:7-9).

This exchange yields an important clue about what Jesus had come to earth to do. Jesus was determined not to lose any of the disciples God had promised to save. He was on a mission to keep his disciples safe. On the night he was arrested, Jesus preserved them by getting his accusers to let them go. They honored this request because Jesus was the only one they wanted. Therefore, while Jesus was dragged away to his trial in chains, his disciples escaped into the darkness, unharmed.

What Jesus did for his disciples that night was an act of friendship. It was the fulfillment of his promise to protect them and keep them safe (John 17:12). But what he did for his disciples the next day was the ultimate sacrifice. If you have heard this story, you know how it ends. After Jesus was tried and convicted, he was tortured and then crucified. The reason he surrendered his body unto death was to save his disciples. It was only by dying for their sins that he could keep them safe for the rest of eternity. Otherwise, they would have to pay for their own sins, in which case they would be lost forever. Jesus died so that his friends could live.

What guarantee do you have for your own safety? The world is not a very safe place. Even if you are never surrounded by soldiers armed to the teeth or victimized by a terrorist attack, you will face dangers of various kinds. Sooner or later you might be mistreated or perhaps even abused. You might have a serious accident. Or perhaps you will be afflicted with a disease. The one thing that is certain is that unless Jesus returns in the meantime, someday you will die. And what will happen to you then?

Christians often talk about being "saved." To be saved is to be rescued from sin and death, and to be delivered from hell, the place of eternal punishment. One way to think about what it means to be saved is to think of the word "safe." To be saved is to be kept safe for all eternity: safe from sin, safe from death, and safe from the wrath of God.

Everyone who comes to Jesus will be kept safe in this way. The Bible says that "he is able to save completely those who come to God through him" (Heb. 7:25). If you ask him to save you, he will keep you safe, as he kept his disciples safe the night that he was arrested, and forever after. For Jesus has made this promise: "I shall lose none of all that he has given me, but raise them up at the last day. For . . . everyone who looks to the Son and believes in him shall have eternal life, and I will raise him up at the last day" (John 6:39-40).

RESISTING ARREST

A person commits a misdemeanor of the second degree if, with the intent of preventing a public servant from effecting a lawful arrest or discharging any other duty, the person creates a substantial risk of bodily injury to the public servant or anyone else, or employs means justifying or requiring substantial force to overcome the resistance.

PENNSYLVANIA CODE 18 PA.C.S.A. § 5104

THREE

THE RESISTANCE

Remember the scene: Having conspired to take Jesus into custody, a rabble of scribes from the Jewish high council and soldiers from the Roman garrison set out for the Garden of Gethsemane. It was the middle of the night. Jesus had been off by himself, saying his prayers. "While he was still speaking, Judas, one of the Twelve, arrived. With him was a large crowd armed with swords and clubs, sent from the chief priests and the elders of the people" (Matt. 26:47).

This much we know already from John's account of Jesus' arrest. Now the Gospel of Matthew adds a significant detail. The "betrayer had arranged a signal with them: 'The one I kiss is the man; arrest him.' Going at once to Jesus, Judas said,

'Greetings, Rabbi!' and kissed him. Jesus replied, 'Friend, do what you came for.' Then the men stepped forward, seized Jesus and arrested him" (Matt. 26:48-50). This traitorous kiss shows how warm an intimacy Jesus shared with his disciples. How often, one wonders, did they press their lips against his beloved cheek? At the same time, it shows how base Judas was in his betrayal. He committed nothing less than a perfidious act of treason.

PETER DRAWS HIS SWORD

The other disciples were not about to let Jesus be captured without a fight. When the unruly mob laid their unholy hands on him, "one of Jesus' companions reached for his sword, drew it out and struck the servant of the high priest, cutting off his ear" (Matt. 26:51). This action clearly falls under the legal category of "resisting arrest," wherein "with the intent of preventing a public servant from effecting a lawful arrest . . . the person creates a substantial risk of bodily injury to the public servant or anyone else."[1] In this case, the person at "substantial risk of bodily injury" was not a public servant but someone else, namely, the servant of the high priest. With one powerful stroke, a disciple of Jesus severed the man's ear from his head.

Given the circumstances, it was a brave thing to do. The Gospel of John mentions that this disciple was Peter (John 18:10), and Luke states that he was not the only disciple who was armed and ready to strike. "When Jesus' followers saw what was going to happen, they said, 'Lord, should we strike with our swords?'" (Luke 22:49). Peter, however, did not wait for permission.

This is not surprising, for Peter was given to impetuous—not to say, foolhardy—behavior. He was the kind of man to strike first and ask questions later. It was Peter who stepped out of the boat and walked on water; Peter who rebuked Jesus when Jesus first predicted his crucifixion; and it was Peter—brave Peter—who promised Jesus, "Even if all fall away on account of you, I never will" (Matt. 26:33). It is not surprising, then, that even though he was vastly outnumbered, Peter drew his sword and struck.

Jesus would have none of it, however. "Put your sword back in its place," Jesus said to him, "for all who draw the sword will die by the sword. Do you think I cannot call on my Father, and he will at once put at my disposal more than twelve legions of angels? But how then would the Scriptures be fulfilled that say it must happen in this way?" (Matt. 26:52-54).

PUT THAT SWORD AWAY!

Jesus put an end to the resistance by giving Peter three good reasons to put his sword back into his belt. The first was that his swordplay was unsafe. Obviously, it was unsafe for the man Peter attacked, although happily he made a speedy recovery! Luke, who as a doctor took a special interest in such matters, records that Jesus "touched the man's ear and healed him" (Luke 22:51).

More to the point, drawing the sword was unsafe for Peter himself. This was not because his swordsmanship was suspect (although cutting off a man's ear was hardly a lethal blow), but because violent men often come to a violent end. As Jesus said, "All who draw the sword will die by the sword" (Matt. 26:52).

Perhaps the best historical example of this comes from the life of Julius Caesar, who was part of the first triumvirate to rule the Republic of Rome. According to the terms of his commission, although Caesar was the military governor of all Gaul, he had no authority over Rome itself. Yet his proud ambition was to defeat his rivals and to reign supreme over the entire Roman Empire. To this end, he amassed troops on the northern border of Italy, on the banks of the River Rubicon. There he received a warning from the Roman Senate that if he set so much as one foot in Italy, he would become an enemy of the Republic. Caesar ignored this warning and crossed the Rubicon, thereby drawing his sword against Rome. He defeated his rivals and satisfied his ambitions. Yet in doing so he brought the Republic to ruin, and in five short years he was slain by the members of his own Senate. When the infamous Brutus drove his dagger into Caesar's chest, the proverb was anticipated: "All who draw the sword will die by the sword."

The Christian church has been painfully slow to learn this lesson. Few things have done more damage to the cause of Christ than misguided attempts to advance his kingdom with the sword. To be sure, the church is engaged in warfare; yet all the weapons in its arsenal are spiritual: truth, righteousness, peace, faith, prayer, "and the sword of the Spirit, which is the word of God" (Eph. 6:17). Nevertheless, Christians have forgotten this and have brought dishonor to Christ by launching unjust crusades and conducting unlawful inquisitions. Rather than resorting to violence, we must heed the words of Christ, who said, "Put your sword back in its place."

In his notes on this passage, the Anglican bishop J. C. Ryle wisely observed:

> The sword has a lawful office of its own. It may be used righteously, in the defence of nations against oppression; it

may become positively necessary to use it, to prevent confusion, plunder, and rapine upon earth: but the sword is not to be used in the propagation and maintenance of the Gospel. Christianity is not to be enforced by bloodshed, and belief in it extorted by force. Happy would it have been for the Church if this sentence had been more frequently remembered! There are few countries in Christendom where the mistake has not been made of attempting to change men's religious opinions by compulsion, penalties, imprisonment, and death. And with what effect? The pages of history supply an answer. No wars have been so bloody as those which have arisen out of the collision of religious opinions: often, mournfully often, the very men who have been most forward to promote those wars have themselves been slain.[2]

THE WAY IT HAD TO BE

Jesus had a second reason for telling Peter to sheath his sword. Not only was it terribly unsafe, but it was also totally unnecessary. Jesus said, "Do you think I cannot call on my Father, and he will at once put at my disposal more than twelve legions of angels?" (Matt. 26:53).

We have already noted that Jesus has a divine nature as well as a human nature. By his divine power, he could have destroyed his enemies in a single instant. Even a glimpse of his heavenly glory would have been enough to drive them all to their knees. But in addition to his own inherent omnipotence, Jesus had the authority to call down the hosts of heaven. At Jesus' request, God the Father would have sent twelve legions of angels to his defense. The term "legion" comes from the Roman army, where a legion was comprised of twelve thousand foot soldiers, plus horsemen. Thus Jesus claimed to have one hundred fifty thousand invincible angels at his command, enough to overpower all the armies on earth. With twelve full legions, Jesus could keep more than ten thousand angels for himself and still have a legion to spare for each of his faithful disciples!

The last thing Jesus needed was someone to defend him. Yet here was Peter, brandishing his sword, whacking off the ear of a lowly servant. He must have looked almost as ridiculous as the mob that had come to make the arrest, armed with their swords and clubs, intending to overpower the Son of God. Jesus even seemed to think that the mob itself was a bit comical: "Am I leading a rebellion," he said, "that you have come out with swords and clubs to capture me?" (Matt. 26:55).

All of this reminds us that Jesus was in total control. It was Jesus who took his disciples to the garden. It was Jesus who said to them, "Look, the hour is near, and the Son of Man is betrayed into the hands of sinners. Rise, let us go! Here comes my betrayer!" (Matt. 26:45b-46). It was Jesus who commanded Judas, "Do what you came for" (Matt. 26:50a). And it was Jesus who allowed himself to be taken into custody. As his case goes to trial, it will become more and more obvious that Jesus was not a passive victim but a willing sacrifice.

This brings us to the third reason Jesus told Peter to put away his sword: his use of the sword went against Scripture. Jesus made this point twice. First he made it in the form of a rhetorical question: "How then would the Scriptures be fulfilled that say it must happen in this way?" (Matt. 26:54). Then he stated it as a foregone conclusion: "This has all taken place that the writings of the prophets might be fulfilled" (Matt. 26:56). In other words, unless he put an end to the resistance, Jesus could never become the Savior God had promised to send.

Jesus was familiar with the Old Testament prophets, who had promised that the Savior would have to suffer and die for sin. He had come to fulfill the prophecy in Isaiah that said he would be "numbered with the transgressors" (Isa. 53:12), so he allowed himself to be arrested like a common criminal. He had come to fulfill the prophecy in Zechariah that said, "Strike the shepherd, and the sheep will be scattered" (Zech. 13:7; cf. Matt. 26:31), so he allowed the soldiers to seize him, and then he watched as "all the disciples deserted him and fled" (Matt. 26:56b). This is the way it happened because, as Jesus knew from Scripture, this is the way it had to be.

NO RESISTANCE

After his disciples left him, Jesus would remain alone for the duration of his trial. Through it all, he offered no resistance. He permitted sinful men to arrest, try, convict, abuse, and execute him. He did not resist because these were the very things he had to suffer for our salvation.

If Peter had understood what Jesus was about to do, he would not have offered any resistance, either. What would you have done? If you had been there when they came to take Jesus away, would you have tried to defend him? Would you have drawn your sword, or would you have run for your life? Perhaps you would have been like Peter, whose first impulse was to defend Jesus. But if you had known what your salvation required, you would have laid down your sword, offering no resistance as Jesus was betrayed and crucified.

Some years ago I attended a play based on the life, death, and resurrection of Jesus Christ. One of the most dramatic scenes came at the end of Jesus' trial before Pilate, when the religious leaders began to call for Jesus to be crucified.

Suddenly, some people sitting in the audience joined the mob, shouting, "Crucify him! Crucify him!" (Matt. 27:22-23). While our attention had been drawn to the action on stage, some of the actors had slipped in from the back of the auditorium and had taken their seats among us. The effect of their shouting was to implicate the audience in the death of Christ. It was as if we ourselves were calling for his crucifixion.

My first impulse was to quiet them down. "No!" I wanted to shout. "Stop! You can't kill him! He's innocent!" But then I remembered that I was a guilty sinner, and that Jesus came to die for my sins too. In that moment I realized that even if I didn't *want* Jesus to be crucified, I *needed* him to be crucified, because my salvation depends upon his cross. And so I laid down my resistance. I took my place in the guilty mob and said in my heart, "Crucify him! Yes, crucify him, if he will be crucified, for I am a sinner who needs a Savior."

WITNESS

In general, one who, being present, personally sees or perceives a thing; a beholder; spectator, or eyewitness. One who testifies to what he has seen, heard or otherwise observed.

BLACK'S LAW DICTIONARY

FOUR

THE WITNESSES

There were many illegalities in Christ's trial, among them the arrest and trial by night, the use of a traitor to identify and secure Jesus, the absence of any formal charge, the rushed one-day duration of the trial, the intervention of the high priest in the proceedings, the lack of a defense, and the unjustified verdict. But underneath these many illegalities ran a strong undercurrent of adherence to certain points of law. Most obvious was the calling of witnesses. Mark indicates what was happening when he records, "The chief priests and the whole Sanhedrin were looking for evidence against Jesus so that they could put him to death, but they did not find any. Many tes-

tified falsely against him, but their statements did not agree"
(Mark 14:55-56).

If this first trial of Jesus, before the Jewish leaders, were
not so evil, one could almost feel sorry for the members of
the Sanhedrin who had gathered. They were clearly unpre-
pared. If they had been prepared, they would have had a formal charge and witnesses ready. As it was, they seem to have
acted only when Judas unexpectedly betrayed Jesus to them.

Most problematic was the matter of witnesses. Where in
Jerusalem in the middle of the night were they to find witnesses to Jesus' alleged crimes? The judges could not be witnesses themselves. Jewish law excluded this possibility.
Witnesses would have to be rounded up from those who might
have heard Jesus say something incriminating. But even if witnesses like this could be found, they would still have to provide evidence according to the strict requirements of Jewish law.

THE SEARCH FOR ADEQUATE TESTIMONY

According to the compendium of Jewish law known as the
Mishnah, there were three categories of testimony: 1) a vain
testimony, 2) a standing testimony, and 3) an adequate testimony. *Vain testimony* referred to accusations that were irrelevant or worthless and could therefore be eliminated at once.

It corresponded to words which in our courts would be "stricken from the record," or which the jury would be instructed to "disregard." *Standing testimony* was testimony that had some relevance to the case and was permitted to stand until it was either confirmed or disproved. *Adequate testimony* was relevant testimony on which two or more witnesses agreed. Only testimony in this third category was sufficient to convict.

Most of the testimony collected in the trial of Jesus, at this late hour, was vain testimony, and there was a great deal of it. Mark says, *"Many* testified falsely against him" (Mark 14:56, emphasis added). A great deal of valuable time—probably hours—was wasted in what we would call a "fishing expedition."

At last two witnesses came with a piece of evidence that put the trial on a promising footing, at least as far as Jesus' enemies were concerned. Mark recorded their testimony: "We heard him say, 'I will destroy this man-made temple and in three days will build another, not made by man'" (Mark 14:58). This was important testimony because, in the first place, apparently it was true. The fact that two witnesses testified to substantially the same thing suggested its truthfulness. In fact, in one of those striking corroborations of one

Gospel by another, John records the incident in which these words were spoken. On the occasion of the first cleansing of the temple, Jesus had replied to the demand for a sign by saying, "Destroy this temple, and I will raise it again in three days" (John 2:19). John does not refer to this in his account of the trial, but he indicates that the words were spoken in the courtyard of the temple, within the hearing of the very types of people who were likely even now to be hanging around the temple in the service of the priests. This was also serious testimony because, if substantiated, it could be construed as sacrilege, since the temple was the most holy place in Israel.

There is something else we should consider, which Frank Morison stresses in his study of Jesus' trial and resurrection.[1] Morison observes that although the saying is reported with variations in wording, the distinctive phrase "in three days" occurs in both Matthew and Mark. This was a phrase Jesus had used on other occasions, in which it was evident that he was prophesying his resurrection, an event that would vindicate his claim to be the unique Son of God. A man as shrewd as the high priest could hardly have been unaware of what Jesus' enigmatic saying implied. He must have understood it perfectly, realizing it was a claim to divinity, and thus in his view a form of blasphemy (even though it was not in a form sufficiently clear to secure the condemnation sought in this trial).

That the religious leaders did understand Jesus' words in this way is proved by an event after the crucifixion. Matthew says that they went to Pilate, saying, "Sir, . . . we remember that while he was still alive that deceiver said, 'After three days I will rise again.' So give the order for the tomb to be made secure until the third day. Otherwise, his disciples may come and steal the body and tell the people that he has been raised from the dead. This last deception will be worse than the first" (Matt. 27:63-64). Clearly, even though they did not believe it, these men understood "after three days" to refer to Jesus' predicted resurrection.

So the situation was this: Jesus was accused of having claimed to be God and of saying that he was able to prove it by rising from the dead. It was a serious accusation, with potentially fatal consequences. Yet strikingly, as important as it was, the testimony of the two witnesses was overthrown. Mark says that this was because "their testimony did not agree" (Mark 14:59). We do not know why, but it was probably due to some minor contradiction. They may have disagreed about the exact place where these words had been spoken. Or they may have reported them with minor variations. After all, the incident had occurred three years earlier.

The high priest must have been so frustrated by this contradiction that he was seething with anger. He understood what Jesus had been claiming. He had a good case, but not good enough to secure a legal verdict. He was right. He was close. Yet the situation was still slipping from his grasp.

THE HIGH PRIEST'S BOLD STROKE

At this point, seeing his case dissolving, the high priest revealed the acumen for which undoubtedly the Romans had made him the chief Jewish ruler. He suddenly turned to the prisoner and demanded, "Are you the Christ, the Son of the Blessed One?" (Mark 14:61). What he did was illegal, because he was forbidden to intervene in a capital trial, and he could only cast his vote after the other court members had cast theirs, but his intervention was brilliant for two reasons. First, for its wording. If he had merely asked whether Jesus was the Messiah, Jesus could have answered "Yes" without jeopardy, for it was not a capital offense to make such a claim. Time would prove it to be either right or wrong. Again, if he had merely asked whether Jesus was the Son of God, Jesus could also have answered "Yes" safely, for he had dealt with a similar accusation earlier by reminding his accusers that many Jews were called "sons of God" (John 10:34-36, quoting Ps. 82:6). However, by linking the two parts as he did, Caiaphas was not asking whether Jesus was the Messiah or a son of God in some general sense, but whether he was the Messiah who was God. If Jesus said "Yes" to that, he could be convicted of the capital crime of blasphemy.

Second, although Jesus was not obliged to give evidence against himself, being a pious Jew he would not refuse answering such a charge. So although he had been silent to this point, Jesus finally spoke up, saying, "I am. . . . And you will see the Son of Man sitting at the right hand of the Mighty One and coming on the clouds of heaven" (Mark 14:62).

At this stage of the trial, when there was no point in remaining silent any longer, Jesus did more than answer the question. He added details as to the kind of Messiah and Son of God he was. He did it by referring to a passage in Daniel where the prophet describes a divine son of man: "There before me was one like a son of man, coming with the clouds of heaven. He approached the Ancient of Days and was led into his presence. He was given authority, glory and sovereign power; all peoples, nations and men of every language

worshiped him. His dominion is an everlasting dominion that
will not pass away, and his kingdom is one that will never be
destroyed" (Dan. 7:13-14).

The judges did not misunderstand that reference. The
high priest tore his clothes. "Why do we need any more witnesses?" he asked. "You have heard the blasphemy. What do
you think?" (Mark 14:63-64). Unanimously they condemned
Jesus as "worthy of death" (Mark 14:64).

A GLARING OMISSION

But hold on a minute! Not so fast! Assuming that a case of
guilt had been made—as it seems to have been, in spite of
the evidence having been illegally obtained—what should
have been the next legal step? Clearly the Sanhedrin should
have begun to inquire into the truth or falsity of the claim. We
might think that the very nature of Jesus' claims would have
put them beyond any meaningful investigation. But that is
not the case. The scribes were masters of the Old Testament.
The elders were charged with the defense of anyone in danger of being put to death. They should have asked whether
Jesus' claims matched what the Old Testament taught concerning the Messiah. If the elders had done this fairly, they
might have discovered that:

1. According to the Scriptures, the Messiah was to have been born in Bethlehem, and Jesus was born in Bethlehem (Mic. 5:2; Luke 2:1-7).

2. The Messiah was to be virgin born, and Jesus was born of Mary, who was a virgin at the time (Isa. 7:14; Matt. 1:24-25; Luke 1:26-30).

3. The Messiah was to be of David's line, and Jesus was descended from King David (2 Sam. 7:12, 16; Isa. 11:1-2; Matt. 1:1-16; Luke 3:23-37).

4. The Messiah was to be preceded by a figure like Elijah, and John the Baptist filled that role (Mal. 3:1; 4:5; Matt. 17:12-13; John 1:19-23).

5. The Messiah was to do many great works, and Jesus had performed the miracles that were prophesied (Isa. 61:1-2; Matt. 11:1-6; Luke 4:16-21).

6. The Messiah was to make a public entry into Jerusalem riding on a donkey, and Jesus had done this just a few days earlier (Zech. 9:9; Matt. 21:1-11; John 12:12-16).

7. The Messiah was to be betrayed by a close friend, and Jesus was so betrayed by Judas (Ps. 41:9; Matt. 26:14-15; 27:3-8).

8. The Messiah was to be despised and rejected by his people, and to become familiar with suffering, as Jesus was (Isa. 53:2-3).

And what about the second part of the accusation, that Jesus had claimed to be God's Son? This was a shocking claim to those who were steeped in the Judaism of Christ's day. It must have been deeply abhorrent. But still, the Sanhedrin could have asked in fairness whether anything of this nature could possibly be suggested by the Scriptures. If they had done this, they might have observed that:

1. There are references in the Old Testament to precisely the kind of unique Son of God Jesus claimed to be (Ps. 2:7; Isa. 9:6).
2. The Old Testament speaks of God becoming flesh (Isa. 7:14).
3. Many Old Testament passages show that the Lord God appeared among men (Gen. 16:13; 18:13, 17, 26; Ex. 3:1-6; Judg. 13; Dan. 3:25).

These passages contain references to the appearances of God on earth in human form, and a fair reading of them would have suggested that Jesus met every reasonable test to determine if he was the Promised One. The Sanhedrin might not have been convinced; probably they would not have been. But this is still a reasonable defense, and its absence from the trial exposes the closed minds and jealous hearts of those who judged Christ.

These leaders were not substantially different from millions of careless people in our day. Christ is proclaimed as God's unique Son, but millions reject that claim and turn their backs on the defense. There is a defense. It is presented regularly in countless Christian churches, on radio and television, and in books, magazines, and other forms of communication. But people will not hear it. They will not go to church. They will not listen to Christian radio. They will not read Christian books. What shall we say of such people? Are they honest? Are they open to the truth? Are they seeking it? No more than the high priest and the other religious leaders of Christ's day.

Yet the important thing is not what others are doing. It is what you are doing. Have you considered Christ's claims? Have you pondered his defense? If not, I challenge you to do it. Because, in the last analysis, it is not Jesus who is on trial. That is over. You are the one who is on trial now, and the question before you is: What will you do with Jesus?

VERDICT

The finding or decision of a Jury, duly sworn and impaneled, after careful consideration, reported to and accepted by the Court.

BLACK'S LAW DICTIONARY

FIVE

THE VERDICT

Jesus was put on trial not once but twice. The Jewish trial, which was an ecclesiastical trial, was held in the middle of the same night that Jesus was betrayed. As we have seen, that trial ended with the high priest convicting him of blasphemy, which was a capital offense.

The second trial, which was a civil trial, began at daybreak. As soon as it was light, "the chief priests, with the elders, the teachers of the law and the whole Sanhedrin . . . bound Jesus, led him away and handed him over to Pilate" (Mark 15:1), the Roman governor. A Roman trial was necessary because the Jews did not have the authority to execute the death penalty. For a crucifixion, they had to appeal to the Romans.

The mention of Pontius Pilate is a reminder that both trials of Jesus were historical events. Whenever Christians recite the Apostles' Creed, they confess their faith in Jesus, "who . . . suffered under Pontius Pilate." This is a way of saying that Jesus was a real person who lived at a particular time in a particular place. To be specific, he was put on trial around 30 A.D., when Pilate was governor of Judea. In the past some scholars doubted whether Pilate ever existed. But in 1961 a team of Italian archaeologists discovered an inscription at Herod's amphitheater in Caesarea that read, "Pontius Pilate, Prefect of Judea, has dedicated to the people of Caesarea a temple in honor of Tiberius."[1]

Archaeologists have also discovered the stone pavement of the very platform where Jesus appeared before Pilate. There they stood, early in the morning: Jesus and Pilate. By the time that trial was over, the scales of justice had been overturned. An innocent man was condemned to die a traitor's death, while the man who sentenced him proved his own guilt, no matter how much he protested his innocence.

WHAT CRIME HAS HE COMMITTED?

The innocent man was Jesus. Salvation itself depends upon this essential fact. Jesus was so completely innocent that his enemies had trouble even coming up with an accusation against him. As John records, when Pilate asked, "What charges are you bringing against this man?" the Jewish leaders answered, "If he were not a criminal, we would not have handed him over to you" (John 18:29-30). It was a clever answer—diabolically clever, alleging that Jesus was a criminal without actually stating the nature of his criminal activity. But Pilate would have none of it. As governor he had the Roman law to uphold, and he was determined to conduct a fair and proper trial. He was unwilling to sentence a man to death without a formal charge.

The prosecution huddled together at this point, trying to come up with something—anything—to get rid of Jesus. In the Jewish trial they had condemned him for blasphemy, but Pilate had no interest in such a fine point of Jewish religious law. So they tried various allegations, trying to make something stick. Finally, they accused Jesus of treason, saying, "We have found this man subverting our nation. He opposes payment of taxes to Caesar and claims to be Christ, a king" (Luke 23:2). "There!" they must have thought. "That will get Pilate's attention!" Blasphemy was one thing, but no one cared more about taxation or revolution than the Romans.

The charge of treason was serious enough at least to arouse the governor's interest. Yet to Pilate's astonishment, Jesus did not try to answer that charge or any of the accusations leveled against him. "Jesus made no reply, not even to a single charge—to the great amazement of the governor" (Matt. 27:14). Pilate was amazed because most of his prisoners did everything they could to save themselves, especially when they were charged with a capital offense like treason. Under Roman law, silence signified consent. If an accused man refused to defend himself, he was assumed to be guilty.

The truth, of course, is that Jesus was innocent, not only of the charge of treason but also of any charge of wrongdoing, for he never committed the least sin. All the biblical writers agree that he was pure and undefiled. Paul referred to Jesus as "him who had no sin" (2 Cor. 5:21). John said, "In him is no sin" (1 John 3:5). Peter claimed, "He committed no sin, and no deceit was found in his mouth" (1 Pet. 2:22). The writer to the Hebrews said that he was "tempted in every way, just as we are—yet was without sin" (Heb. 4:15). Jesus had to be without sin in order to become the Savior.

But in order to be the Savior, Jesus also had to die for sinners, which is why he did not protest his innocence. The famous trial lawyer Johnnie Cochrane once was asked whom he would have preferred to defend. "Jesus is the person I would like to have defended," Cochrane said. "I would have relished the opportunity to defend someone who was completely innocent of all charges and a victim of religious persecution. However, because of his mission here, he would have undoubtedly declined."[2]

Johnnie Cochrane was right. Innocent though he was, Jesus had no interest in mounting a defense. If he had wanted to, he could have summoned witnesses to testify that he always paid his taxes and that he never advocated overthrowing the Roman government. But he just stood there, silent. By in essence pleading no contest, Jesus knew that he was guaranteeing his own execution. But he was on a mission he could not accomplish unless he was sentenced to die. He had come to offer himself as the perfect sacrifice for sin.

I AM INNOCENT OF THIS MAN'S BLOOD!

Jesus was such a perfect man that even Pontius Pilate knew he was innocent. Pilate is often blamed for putting Jesus to death. And rightly so! In the end, it was his verdict that sent Jesus to the cross. But it is seldom recognized how hard Pilate worked to get Jesus released. He tried every means he could think of to get him acquitted and discharged.

In a legal situation such as this one, the powers of the Roman governor were broad. He served as both judge and jury, conducting his own investigation and rendering his own verdict. And unlike the high priest, he had the prerogative to question the accused. Therefore, once Pilate heard the charges, he interrogated Jesus. It did not take him long to realize that Jesus was completely innocent. Pilate knew revolutionaries when he saw them, and it was obvious that Jesus was no revolutionary, at least not in the political sense.

Pilate was also well used to dealing with the Jewish scribes, and he recognized that "it was out of envy that they had handed Jesus over to him" (Matt. 27:18). Since when had the Jews ever been concerned about people not paying their taxes to Rome? Not only did Pilate know that Jesus was innocent, but his wife knew it too: "While Pilate was sitting on the judge's seat, his wife sent him this message: 'Don't have anything to do with that innocent man, for I have suffered a great deal today in a dream because of him'" (Matt. 27:19).

Jesus was so obviously innocent that his hearing before Pilate turned out to be not much of a trial. It consisted mainly of Pilate trying to find a maneuver that would enable him to set Jesus free. First he tried sending the matter back to the Jewish court: "Take him yourselves and judge him by your own law" (John 18:31a). That strategy failed because the Jewish leaders were determined to have Jesus executed, which was not within their power. Next Pilate remanded Jesus into the custody of King Herod, because during the trial Pilate learned that Jesus was from Galilee, which was then under Herod's jurisdiction. But Herod quickly returned Jesus to Pilate, and the governor was right back where he had started.

Still seeking a maneuver that would get the prisoner off, Pilate urged Jesus to defend himself. But Jesus refused, and Pilate was still getting nowhere. Then he remembered that it was his custom during Passover to release a prisoner chosen by the crowd. "So when the crowd had gathered, Pilate asked them, 'Which one do you want me to release to you: Barabbas, or Jesus who is called Christ?'" (Matt. 27:17). It must have seemed like a winning strategy. Surely the crowd would ask for Jesus. Barabbas was a low-life terrorist, while Jesus was a religious leader with plenty of popular support. In fact, that was why the Jewish leaders were so jealous of him. Yet Pilate's ploy turned out to be a tactical blunder: the people surprised him by calling for Barabbas to be set free.

Even at this point, the verdict was still undecided. "'What shall I do, then, with Jesus who is called Christ?' Pilate asked. They all answered, 'Crucify him!'" (Matt.

27:22). Still the governor remained unconvinced that Jesus deserved to die, but he did have him scourged (John 19:1). Such torture was a lighter sentence than crucifixion, but severe enough, and Pilate hoped that it would quench the mob's thirst for blood. Many Roman victims were whipped to the bone, and some actually died. When the soldiers then brought out Jesus, battered and bloodied, Pilate appealed to the crowd: "'Look, I am bringing him out to you to let you know that I find no basis for a charge against him.' When Jesus came out wearing the crown of thorns and the purple robe, Pilate said to them, 'Here is the man!'" (John 19:4-5). But the chief priests and the other officials were not out just for blood; they wanted the death penalty. "Crucify!" they shouted. "Crucify!" (John 19:6a).

By this time, Pilate was even willing to take up Jesus' defense. "Why?" he asked. "What crime has he committed?" (Matt. 27:23). But that only made the mob shout even louder. "Crucify him! Crucify him!" (Matt. 27:22-23). Finally, having exhausted all his options, the governor washed his hands of the whole affair. "When Pilate saw that he was getting nowhere, but that instead an uproar was starting, he took water and washed his hands in front of the crowd. 'I am innocent of this man's blood,' he said. 'It is your responsibility!' All the people answered, 'Let his blood be on us and on our children!' Then he released Barabbas to them. But he had Jesus flogged, and handed him over to be crucified" (Matt. 27:24-26).

BEHOLD THE MAN!

In a recent biography of Pontius Pilate, Ann Wroe identifies the infamous governor as "a symbol of . . . all men facing, considering and ultimately rejecting the truth. . . . [People] love to watch him. . . . In some sense, they feel they are watching themselves."[3] It is true; we do see a great deal of ourselves in Pilate. He was pressured into making the wrong choice, and we ourselves face the same pressures, struggling to uphold our convictions against friends, family members, or the general public. Sometimes, like Pilate, we play to the crowd. And often, like Pilate, we are much quicker to blame others than we are to take responsibility for our own actions. Instead of claiming that he was innocent and that the Jews were guilty, Pontius Pilate should have confessed that all humans are guilty and that Christ alone is innocent.

Pilate made the wrong choice, and he will be judged accordingly. There is a sense in which he himself was on trial, for God will judge Pilate on the basis of the verdict he gave

Jesus. This is true for everyone: God will judge us on the basis of our decision about Jesus Christ. Thus the trial of Jesus has a way of putting *us* on trial. We are forced to reach a verdict on Jesus; and God, in turn, judges us on the basis of that verdict.

So what do you think of Jesus? You may not hate him the way the scribes did. Make no mistake, they wanted Jesus to be damned. Since hanging on a tree was a sign of God's curse (Deut. 21:22-23), by calling for his crucifixion they were trying to send him to hell. If you had such animosity toward Jesus, it is doubtful whether you would be reading this book. But you do not have to hate Jesus to reject him. Pontius Pilate is the perfect example. Obviously, the man had some respect for Jesus. He did almost everything he could to help him. But in the end Pilate sent Jesus away, and thus he was lost in his sins. No matter how hard he scrubbed his hands with water, he would never be able to wash himself clean. Only Jesus can wash away sin, but he is the very one whom Pilate rejected.

In a strange way, Pilate's own words confirmed that Jesus is the Savior. First he announced that he could find no basis for a charge against Jesus, in effect declaring him innocent. Ultimately, this would help the whole world know that when

Jesus died, he was a perfectly sinless sacrifice. Nevertheless, Pilate condemned Jesus to die. This showed how, in keeping with God's plan of salvation, Jesus took our sins upon himself. The innocent was declared guilty so that the guilty could be declared innocent. Now, everyone who trusts in Jesus receives the forgiveness of sins through his perfect sacrifice. Really, the only way Pilate could have washed his hands of anything was to believe in Jesus. Yet sadly, as far as his own personal faith commitment was concerned, the governor reached the wrong verdict on Jesus.

What is your verdict? There is a famous nineteenth-century painting by Ciseri called *Ecce Homo.* The painting, which hangs in the Palazzo Pitti Gallery in Florence, is based on Jesus' trial before Pilate. It takes its title from Pilate's words to the crowd: "Behold the man!" (John 19:5, KJV) or in Latin, *Ecce Homo!* In the painting, Jesus stands on the terrace, stripped to the waist, his hands bound behind him; Pilate stands in the middle of the painting, with his back to the viewer. He is leaning forward, head bent over the railing, appealing to the masses gathered below him in the streets. With one hand he gestures toward Jesus, as if to ask, "What will you do with him?"

It is a question every person must answer. Here is the

man—the God-Man—Jesus Christ. He is the most perfect, the most innocent man who ever lived. The Bible claims that he offered his life as a perfect sacrifice for sin, and that everyone who believes in him will receive eternal life. You can try to send him away, pushing him out of your thoughts, but he will always come back to mind. You will never be able to wash your hands of him. God will always hold you responsible for your decision about Jesus Christ.

Behold the Man! What will you do with him?

SENTENCE

The judgment formally pronounced by the Court or Judge upon the defendant after his conviction in a criminal prosecution, imposing the punishment to be inflicted.

BLACK'S LAW DICTIONARY

SIX

THE SENTENCE

Pilate condemned Jesus to die on the cross, even though it was against his better judgment. His own personal verdict was that Jesus was innocent of all the charges against him. "I have examined him in your presence," he said to the Jewish leaders, "and have found no basis for your charges against him. . . . [A]s you can see, he has done nothing to deserve death" (Luke 23:14b, 15b).

At first Pilate was adamant, saying, "I have found in him no grounds for the death penalty" (Luke 23:22). But as the mob grew more and more frantic, Pilate gave in to their bloodthirsty demands. Although he never pronounced a legal verdict against Jesus, or handed down a proper death sentence, make no mistake: he did condemn Jesus to die. The Bible simply says, "Finally Pilate handed him over to them to be crucified" (John 19:16).

CRUCIFY HIM!

Although ultimately it was Pilate who gave Jesus his death sentence, it was really the religious leaders who insisted on it. This is most clearly recorded in the Gospel of John:

> When Jesus came out wearing the crown of thorns and the purple robe, Pilate said to them, "Here is the man!" As soon as the chief priests and their officials saw him, they shouted, "Crucify! Crucify!" But Pilate answered, "You take him and crucify him. As for me, I find no basis for a charge against him." The Jews insisted, "We have a law, and according to that law he must die, because he claimed to be the Son of God" (John 19:5-7).

That last statement indicates what some consider to be the legal basis of the death sentence against Jesus. According to the Jewish religious leaders, Jesus had to die because he said that he was the Son of God. In their view this was blasphemy, which carried the death penalty under Jewish law.

As we saw in chapter 5, the religious leaders had to convince Pilate to ratify the death sentence. To persuade the governor that Jesus deserved to die, they brought a total of six charges against him. The first was made during the ecclesiastical trial before the Sanhedrin, where they charged Jesus with threatening to destroy the Jewish temple (Matt. 26:61). The other five charges were brought against Jesus in his political trial before Pilate. They accused Jesus of criminal wrongdoing (John 18:30), of subverting the nation (Luke 23:2), of forbidding the Jews to pay their taxes to Caesar (Luke 23:2), of stirring up rebellion among the people (Luke 23:5), and of claiming to be the king (Luke 23:2-3).

These were all serious charges, but they were not the real reason that the Jewish leaders hated Jesus and had brought him before Pilate. The real accusation for them was that Jesus had claimed to be the unique Son of God. This was their seventh and central accusation. It had been there from the beginning, of course. The very first accusation against Jesus was that he claimed he was "able to destroy the temple of God and rebuild it in three days" (Matt. 26:61). The leaders of Israel undoubtedly read into Jesus' words precisely what was intended, that he was God and that, although he would permit the leaders of the nation to kill him, he would rise again in three days.

Why, then, were the other charges raised? They were raised because Jesus' enemies knew that the Roman governor would never consent to convict Christ on a point of Jewish religious law. Before Pilate, Jesus had to be accused of insurrection. Thus up to this point Pilate had been conducting the trial as if Jesus were only a man and the issues were merely human. As far as he was concerned, the crux of the matter lay in his challenge: "Behold the *man!*" Now the ground shifted completely. Pilate had to face the entirely new question as to whether Jesus was actually the Son of God.

Was Jesus' claim to be the Son of God factual? I ask the question because it is not only Pilate who is forced to face this question. You must confront it too.

AS GOD IS MY WITNESS

When Donald Grey Barnhouse preached on the trial of Jesus, he asked the question this way: "Who died at Calvary?"[1] In his sermon Dr. Barnhouse pointed out that the question is not as easy as it seems. It cannot be answered simply by saying that the man who was sentenced to crucifixion was Jesus of Nazareth, because there is no question about that. The question is: Who was Jesus? Was he merely a man? Or was he in fact God, as he claimed to be? The Jewish leaders disputed this claim, but the question still needs to be resolved: Who died at Calvary?[2]

Dr. Barnhouse called witnesses to help adjudicate the matter. The most important witness to any fact is *God himself.* Here we forego the numerous Old Testament prophecies concerning the Messiah (some of these were listed in chapter 4) and turn instead to the testimony God rendered during the days of Christ's earthly ministry. We turn to the moment of Christ's baptism. We hear God speak, saying, "This is my Son, whom I love; with him I am well pleased" (Matt. 3:17). Has such a testimony ever been rendered to another? Here is one called God's Son. The testimony is weighty.

Next we turn to that moment toward the end of Christ's ministry when he stands on the Mount of Transfiguration and is changed from his earthly into his heavenly appearance. He is clothed with light as with a garment, and in the hearing of Peter, James, and John, God Almighty says again from heaven, "This is my Son, whom I love; with him I am well pleased. Listen to him!" (Matt. 17:5). God the Father testified to Christ's deity.

The second witness to be summoned is *Jesus of Nazareth.* Any court should be willing to hear a man's testimony about himself. So we turn to Jesus and press our question on him. His reply goes something like this:

> I have already given my testimony. On one occasion the leaders of Israel challenged me to give an accounting of myself, and I did this so clearly (saying, "Before Abraham was born, I am!" [John 8:58]) that they immediately tried to stone me. On another occasion I taught in Solomon's porch, saying, "I and the Father are one" (John 10:30), and again they wanted to stone me. Just this week, in my final moments with my disciples, I answered Philip's question, saying, "Anyone who has seen me has seen the Father" (John 14:9). And last night when the high priest asked, "Are you the Christ, the Son of the Blessed One?" I replied, "I am! And you will see the Son of Man sitting at the right hand of the Mighty One and coming on the clouds of heaven" (Mark 14:61-62). It is for this claim that I am being tried and for which I will be sentenced to die.

We have heard the witness of two persons of the Trinity. But what about the *Holy Spirit?* Before his arrest, Jesus had said of the Holy Spirit, "When the Counselor comes, whom I will send to you from the Father, the Spirit of truth who goes out from the Father, he will testify about me" (John 15:26). And this the Spirit has done in the pages of the Scriptures that he inspired. The entire New Testament, in fact, is the Spirit's witness to Jesus Christ. Thus the Father, the Son, and the Holy Spirit all testify to the deity of Jesus Christ.

THE TESTIMONY OF MEN AND WOMEN

It is not only supernatural witnesses but also human ones who attest to Christ's deity, and among them are some who knew him best. What of these men and women? What, for example, of the writers of the Gospels? These men were the historians of Christ's life. They may rightly be supposed to have carefully investigated the things that were being said about him. Some even lived or traveled with him. They were eyewitnesses of the events they described. What do these men think of the One who stands before Pilate?

Matthew, what do you think? You wrote one of our Gospels. You are a Jew, and the Jews confess one God. You are not likely to ascribe divinity to any man without over-whelming evidence.

Matthew replies, "I believe that Jesus is the divine Savior of whom the Old Testament speaks. I have said so publicly. I said that his birth was in fulfillment of that great prophecy of Isaiah, which says, 'The virgin will be with child and will give birth to a son, and they will call him Immanuel . . . God with us'" (Matt. 1:23; cf. Isa. 7:14).

Mark, what about you? You traveled with Peter. You received firsthand information about Jesus from him. What do you think?

Mark answers that he too is on record, having introduced his Gospel with these words: "The beginning of the gospel about Jesus Christ, the Son of God" (Mark 1:1).

Luke, what about you? You're a physician. You are not inclined to flights of fancy or exaggeration. We'd like to hear from you, too.

Luke replies that he has given us the most scientific language of the four Gospels, and that he has recorded some of the most exalted titles ever given to Jesus: "Son of the Most High" (Luke 1:32); "Son of God" (Luke 1:35); and "Christ the Lord" (Luke 2:11).

And *John,* what's your testimony? We know that you were very close to Jesus.

John replies that he has written the most explicit words of all, stating, "In the beginning was the Word, and the Word was with God, and the Word was God. He was with God in the beginning. Through him all things were made; without him nothing was made that has been made. In him was life, and that life was the light of men" (John 1:1-4). He adds that he is also on record as saying, "Jesus did many other miraculous signs in the presence of his disciples, which are not recorded in this book. But these are written that you may believe that Jesus is the Christ, the Son of God, and that by believing you may have life in his name" (John 20:30-31).

There are other human witnesses as well. There is *John the Baptist,* the first cousin of Jesus, who said, "I have seen and I testify that this is the Son of God" (John 1:34). There is *Martha,* in whose home Jesus and his disciples often stayed. To Jesus she said, "I believe that you are the Christ, the Son of God, who was to come into the world" (John 11:27). And when Jesus once asked the disciples, "Who do you say I am?" *Peter,* speaking for the rest, declared, "You are the Christ, the Son of the living God" (Matt. 16:15-16).

Did Jesus reject any of these confessions? He certainly could have, but he never did. If ever there was an opportunity to correct a "mistaken" notion of who he was, Jesus could have said to Peter, "You are wrong, Peter. I am not God's Son. I am just a man, as you are." Instead he replied, "Blessed are you, Simon son of Jonah, for this was not revealed to you by man, but by my Father in heaven" (Matt. 16:17).

WHAT IS YOUR VERDICT?

The earthly and the heavenly witnesses agree. Jesus of Nazareth is exactly who he claimed to be: the Son of God. Sadly, when the Jewish leaders rejected this claim, they were rejecting the very Son of God. Even worse, they actively sought to have him sentenced to death by crucifixion. And what of Pontius Pilate? By washing his hands of the whole affair, he too rejected the deity of Jesus Christ and the salvation that can only be found in him.

Here we must leave the trial of Jesus behind and come at last to ourselves. We have not seen Jesus in the days of his flesh, but he is proclaimed to us in Scripture, and the Holy Spirit bears witness to him in countless Christian hearts. What do we say? Is he the Son of God?

I give you *my testimony.* When I look within my heart, I know that there is nothing within me to draw me to him. He is a thing apart. Left to myself, I would find a lifetime of other pursuits to keep me busy. I could be as skeptical as Thomas or as hostile as the apostle Paul before his conversion. But Jesus spoke to me. He spoke through the Word of God, declaring who he is and what he has done. My heart went out to him, and I confess that he is indeed the Son of God, and my Savior.

Is that *your testimony?* You have heard the evidence. Will you decide in favor of his claims? Or will you decide against him? The strange thing about this case is that the decision you make will not determine the destiny of the defendant. It will determine the destiny of yourself, the judge.

EXECUTION

The carrying out of a death sentence.

SEVEN

THE EXECUTION

We have followed the trial of Jesus Christ through six stages: 1) the conspiracy to kill him; 2) the arrest in the garden; 3) the futile resistance by Peter; 4) the witnesses at the trial before the Jewish Sanhedrin; 5) the verdict of the Roman governor Pontius Pilate; and 6) the sentence of death that led at once to the crucifixion. In this last chapter we come to the crucifixion itself.

The Gospels tell us that Jesus was led to the place of execution, carrying his cross according to the Roman custom, and that he was crucified between two thieves who had been condemned at about the same time. A placard was nailed above the cross specifying the crime for which Jesus was being executed. The placard read "JESUS OF NAZARETH, THE KING OF THE JEWS" (John 19:19b). Then the people and their leaders gathered around the cross to mock Jesus, as crowds often will mock someone less fortunate than themselves. "He saved others, but he can't save himself!" (Mark 15:31), they said, "Let this Christ, this King of Israel, come down now from the cross, that we may see and believe" (Mark 15:31-32).

But this is precisely what Jesus would not do. Physically it was possible, of course. All Jesus had to do was call on the angels of heaven and they would have come instantly to rescue him. As we have noted earlier, when Jesus was arrested in the garden, he told his disciples that if he had asked, his Father would have put at his disposal "more than twelve legions of angels" (Matt. 26:53). But Jesus could not do that and at the same time make atonement for his people, which is why he came to earth in the first place.

THE MIRACLES OF CALVARY

All the Gospels report Jesus' death. It is the chief reason they were written. The atoning death and victorious resurrection of Jesus are the heart of the gospel story. But the four Gospels differ in their reports of the details that accompanied Jesus' death. John, the author of the fourth Gospel, was concerned about the Scriptures that were fulfilled at the time. The first three Gospels do not refer to those parts of Scripture. Instead they report several surprising signs or miracles that occurred when Jesus died.

Matthew's account of these miracles is the most complete. He tells of four miracles: 1) the darkening of the sky between noon and three in the afternoon while Jesus was on the cross; 2) the tearing of the veil of the temple from top to bottom when Jesus died; 3) the earthquake that opened many of the tombs near the place of the crucifixion; and 4) the resurrection to life of many holy people who had died. The accounts in Mark and Luke are briefer. They record that the land grew dark and that the veil of the temple was torn, ending with the words of the Roman centurion who stood at the foot of the cross: "Surely this man was the Son of God!" (Mark 15:39; cf. Matt. 27:54; Luke 23:47). In a way, these words also represented a miracle—the miracle of a sinner coming to faith in Christ.

It is not surprising that miracles accompanied the death of Jesus, since they also accompanied his birth. But most of us do not think about them very often. We talk about the birth miracles: the virgin birth itself, the angel visitations, the star

that guided the wise men. But we do not pay much attention to the death miracles. Why? Probably because Jesus'
death was followed by his resurrection, which is the most
significant miracle of all. Nevertheless, the other miracles
teach us about the meaning of the death of Jesus. In particular, they show what verdict God himself reached concerning
Jesus and his trial.

DARKNESS AMID THE BLAZE OF NOON

There are two miracles in Mark's account. He reports that
"at the sixth hour darkness came over the whole land until
the ninth hour" (Mark. 15:33). That the sky should grow
dark during the day is not in itself miraculous or even odd.
We have all seen the sky grow dark when a particularly
severe storm is approaching. Volcanic eruptions can also
cause darkness. The sky grew dark over Pompeii in 79 A.D.
when Vesuvius erupted, and the same thing happened in
1980 when Mount St. Helens erupted in Washington State.
And an eclipse of the sun can cause darkness of a sort. But
there are no volcanoes in Israel, it seldom rains, and this was
not an eclipse. A full eclipse lasts only a few minutes, but
this darkness lasted for three hours. No, this was a special
divine intervention in the normal workings of nature, by

which the sky grew dark from noon until three in the afternoon, when Jesus cried with a loud voice and gave up his spirit.

This darkness must have been a striking, sober, and well-observed phenomenon. Tertullian, an early Christian apologist, referred to this darkness when he reminded his heathen readers that the "wonder is related in your own annals and is preserved in your archives to this day." But it is remarkable how restrained Matthew, Mark, and Luke are as they report it. They do not embellish the story or speculate about the source of the darkness. In a manner that can only enhance their credibility as historians, each simply reports that at the sixth hour darkness came over the whole land until the ninth hour (Matt. 27:45; Mark 15:33; Luke 23:44).

These dark hours represent a gap in the narrative, a time about which we know almost nothing. But there was much going on before the darkness descended. Jesus had prayed for the soldiers who were crucifying him. He had spoken words of promise to the believing criminal hanging beside him. He had commended his mother to the care of the beloved disciple. The chief priests, the teachers of the law, and the elders had been taunting him. But with the descent of the darkness the narrative ceases, as if a veil had been drawn over the unspeakable suffering of God's Son.

What happened during those hours of darkness? We know the answer. It was in those hours that the Son of God took the burden of our sins upon himself, was punished for them in our place, and experienced such terrible alienation from his Father that he cried out, *"Eloi, Eloi, lama sabachthani?"* which means, "My God, my God, why have you forsaken me!" (Mark 15:34). During those hours, God was carrying out his judgment against human sin, giving it the death sentence it deserved. The darkness thus veiled the anguish of the Son of God while he was bearing the punishment for our sins; it was not right for human eyes to look upon him in his suffering. At the same time, the darkness testified to the blackness of our sin and the tremendous cost to God of our redemption.

THE TEARING OF THE VEIL

Another miracle that took place at the time of Jesus' death was the tearing in two of the great veil that separated the Holy Place from the Most Holy Place in the temple. Matthew, Mark, and Luke report this. Matthew and Mark add that it was torn in two "from top to bottom" (Matt.

27:51; Mark 15:38), suggesting that this was something God did.

To understand the spiritual significance of this miracle, we must know something about the placement and function of this veil. The very word *veil* means "to hide" or "cover," and in this case the veil was used to hide the innermost recesses of the temple, which contained the ark of the covenant. The temple area was designed as a series of courts, in the center of which was the temple building itself, which was divided into two parts. The first and larger part was the Holy Place. The other and smaller part was called the Most Holy Place. Separating the two parts, or rooms, was the veil of which the Gospel writers speak. In the early days of Israel's history, before the destruction of the temple by the Babylonians, this innermost room contained the ark of the covenant with its mercy seat, where God was understood to dwell in a symbolic sense. The presence of God above the ark in the Most Holy Place testified to the presence of God with his people.

This veil thus pointed to the enormous gulf that exists between God in his holiness and us in our depravity. It was a way of saying symbolically, but also unmistakably, "Thus far you may come, but no farther." There was only one day in the year when the veil could be passed, and that was on the Day of Atonement, when the high priest took the blood of an animal that had been killed moments before in the court-yard into the temple, carried it past the veil, and then sprin-kled it on the mercy seat of the ark. The mercy seat was the ark's cover or lid. On it were figures of two angels who faced each other and whose wings stretched backward and upward and almost touched at the top. That made a space in which God was understood to dwell in a symbolic way. Within the ark, below the space where God was thought to dwell, were the two tables of the law.

The ark of the covenant was for Israel a picture of judg-ment. The righteous, holy God of the universe looked down on the law, knowing that it had been broken, and that he must punish the people for their sin. This dramatic illustration was a constant reminder of God's verdict against his people's sin. But when the high priest sprinkled blood on the mercy seat, the blood came between God and the broken law. This act indicated that atonement had been made for sin. An inno-cent victim (the sacrificed animal) had died in the people's place, so that rather than pouring forth wrath, God could shower his people with grace and mercy. This pointed forward to the true and final atonement that Jesus Christ would make by dying on the cross.

Here we see the significance of the torn veil. It shows that when Jesus died, everything to which the Old Testament sacrifices pointed was fulfilled. There is no need for any further sacrifice for sin. God has accepted the sacrifice of his Son as the full payment for sin. The death penalty has been fully executed, and now the way to God is open for all who would put their trust in Jesus. God showed this dramatically by tearing the veil from top to bottom.

Significantly, the veil was torn at three in the afternoon, which was the time for the evening sacrifice. The priests would have been in the temple, engaged in their duties, when the veil was torn. They would have seen it— no doubt standing aghast before the innermost recess of the temple, now exposed—and they should have known that the age in which they had served was now over and a new age of God's dealings with his people had begun. This may help explain something we read later in Acts (and which we saw in chapter 1): "So the word of God spread. The number of disciples in Jerusalem increased rapidly, and *a large number of priests* became obedient to the faith" (Acts 6:7, emphasis added).

THE LESSONS OF THE VEIL

There are several lessons to learn from the tearing of the veil. First, the old system of offering sacrifices year by year is over. It is hard for us to appreciate how many sacrifices were made on a regular basis at the temple. The offering of blood that the high priest made on the Day of Atonement was only one of many sacrifices.

The book of Leviticus lists the various offerings, such as a burnt offering, which was an offering for sin. It could be a large animal like a sheep or goat, or a small animal like a young pigeon. It was called a burnt offering because it was consumed entirely on the altar. Another offering was a fellowship offering. Part of this offering was burnt, but the worshiper and his family ate the rest, which is why it was called a fellowship offering. These offerings went on every single day, plus there were special offerings for special days. After the temple veil was torn during the crucifixion, the priests probably sewed the pieces back together and went on with their age-old rituals. But in the sight of God, the old age had ended and a new age had begun.

Second, Jesus' offering of himself was the perfect and final sacrifice for sin. Therefore, nothing more needs to be done or can be done to reconcile sinful men and women to God.

Jesus' sacrifice of himself was a real sacrifice for sin, not a symbol that merely pointed forward to something else, as the Old Testament sacrifices did. The Old Testament sacrifices pointed forward to the atonement Jesus would make, but they were not themselves that atonement. Jesus put away our real sin by his real death. To suggest that anything more is necessary for salvation is to deny the doctrine known as *solus Christus* (Christ alone), which expresses the completeness and total sufficiency of Christ's work.

The author of the book of Hebrews says very clearly, "[Christ did not] enter heaven to offer himself again and again, the way the high priest enters the Most Holy Place every year with blood that is not his own. Then Christ would have had to suffer many times since the creation of the world. But now he has appeared once for all at the end of the ages to do away with sin by the sacrifice of himself. Just as man is destined to die once, and after that to face judgment, so Christ was sacrificed once to take away the sin of many people, and he will appear a second time, not to bear sin, but to bring salvation to those who are waiting for him" (Heb. 9:25-28). This is why today we insist that there is no Savior but Jesus and that we must believe on him and commit ourselves to him if we are to be saved.

THE LAST MIRACLE

Because of Christ's saving work, it is now possible for those who believe on him to approach God directly. The people of God could not do this before Christ's death. They needed to approach God indirectly, asking a priest to intercede for them. But now the way is open for everybody. The author of Hebrews wrote, "Therefore, brothers, since we have confidence to enter the Most Holy Place by the blood of Jesus, by a new and living way opened for us through the curtain, that is, his body, and since we have a great priest over the house of God, let us draw near to God with a sincere heart in full assurance of faith. . . . Let us hold unswervingly to the hope we profess, for he who promised is faithful" (Heb. 10:19-23).

Remarkably, as we have seen, one man who approached God by faith was the Roman centurion standing at the foot of the cross when Jesus was crucified. Presumably he was the leader of those who had been given the task of executing Pilate's death sentence against Jesus. We can assume that the man was a pagan, but by the miraculous power of God's Spirit, he was quickened to spiritual life. We know this because when the centurion and those with him saw Jesus die on the cross, they cried out with true faith, "Surely he was the Son of God!" (Matt. 27:54).

This may not have been a full confession. It lacked much that the centurion undoubtedly would come to know later. But it was correct as far as it went, and Matthew included it as an example of what is required of all who come face to face with Jesus. Have you made that vital confession, acknowledging that Jesus is both the Son of God and your Savior? You need to. It is the only way that anyone can be saved.

AFTERWORD

There is something that you should know about the last chapter of this book: it comes from almost the last sermon that James Boice ever preached. He preached it on Good Friday 2000, just hours after learning from his doctor that he had an aggressive and ultimately fatal form of liver cancer.

It has been observed that a great minister "preaches as a dying man to dying men." This was always true of James Boice, but never more so than on the last Good Friday of his thirty-two-year ministry in the pulpit of Tenth Presbyterian Church. It was true again just two days later, on Easter Sunday, when Dr. Boice preached his last weekly sermon: "The Difference a Day Makes."

That sermon was important because it completed the story of Jesus and his trial. Even crucifixion was not the end for Jesus, because three days later he rose again. As Dr. Boice explained in that final sermon, the first Christians proclaimed in Jesus the resurrection of the dead. Speaking to the very leaders who had carried out the crucifixion, they identified Jesus as the man "whom you crucified but whom God raised from the dead" (Acts 4:10). The crucifixion and the resurrection—these were the central points of their teaching.

Furthermore, by raising Jesus from the dead, God announced his own verdict on his Son, declaring that by his death he had fully satisfied the penalty for sin. Dr. Boice said: "Easter proves that Jesus is God, that he is the Savior, that death is not the end for anyone, that there is a resurrection. Thus Jesus' resurrection proves everything that is essential about Christianity." All this was proven the day that Jesus rose from the dead. What a difference a day makes!

James Boice died less than two months after preaching his last Easter sermon. Death always brings disappointment. In the present context, it is regrettable that he and I were unable to complete our full plan of sermons on the trial of Jesus. We had hoped to preach a series of messages called "Overturned on Appeal." These would have focused on New Testament texts in which God the Father vindicates the work of his Son, especially his death on the cross for sinners. We would have completed our preaching program with "Judge over All," seven sermons on the role of Jesus at the final judgment.

Undoubtedly we would have ended with a question that

has been raised throughout *Jesus on Trial,* and that I am compelled to ask again. God has promised that one day Jesus will come back to this earth. This time he will not come as a defendant to be tried by unjust men. He will not come to be judged at all, but only to judge. So the question is this: Are you ready for the final judgment, the trial of your life?

Be assured that you will not be declared innocent on the basis of your own record. The only safety for all eternity is faith in Jesus Christ. He is the only man who is perfectly innocent, and his death in the place of guilty sinners is the only hope of salvation there is.

Philip Graham Ryken
Tenth Presbyterian Church
October 2001

NOTES

CHAPTER 1: THE CONSPIRACY

1. Plato, *The Republic of Plato,* trans. Francis MacDonald Cornford (London: Oxford University Press, 1945), 46-47.
2. Pennsylvania Code 18 Pa.C.S.A. § 903(a).
3. Vinoth Ramachandra, *Gods That Fail* (Downers Grove, Ill.: InterVarsity, 1996), 200.
4. Jacob Revius, "He Bore Our Griefs," trans. Henrietta Ten Harmsel.

CHAPTER 2: THE ARREST

1. Alexander Maclaren, *Expositions of Holy Scripture,* 11 vols. (Grand Rapids, Mich.: Eerdmans, 1959), 7:221.
2. Frank Morison, *Who Moved the Stone?* (London, 1930; repr. Grand Rapids, Mich.: Zondervan, 1958), 33.

CHAPTER 3: THE RESISTANCE

1. Pennsylvania Code 18 Pa.C.S.A. § 5104.
2. John Charles Ryle, *Expository Thoughts on the Gospels: St. Matthew* (Cambridge: James Clarke, 1974), 368.

CHAPTER 4: THE WITNESSES

1. Frank Morison, *Who Moved the Stone?* (1930; repr. Grand Rapids, Mich.: Zondervan, 1958), 24.

CHAPTER 5: THE VERDICT

1. John McRay, *Archaeology and the New Testament* (Grand Rapids, Mich.: Baker, 1991), 145.
2. Johnnie Cochrane, *Time* (June 29, 1998), 25.
3. Ann Wroe, *Pilate: The Biography of an Invented Man* (London: Jonathan Cape, 1999), 217-218.

CHAPTER 6: THE SENTENCE

1. Donald Grey Barnhouse, *Eternity* (April 1962), 9-11.
2. Much of the material in this chapter first appeared in James Montgomery Boice, "Who Died on Calvary?" *The Gospel of John, Volume 5: Triumph Through Tragedy, John 18–21* (Grand Rapids, Mich.: Baker, 1999), 1471-1476.

INDEX OF NAMES

SCRIPTURE INDEX